THE HINDRANCES OF A HOUSEHOLDER

THE HINDRANCES OF A HOUSEHOLDER

JENNIFER BARTLETT

CHAX
2018

ISBN 978-1-946104-08-3

Chax Press
PO Box 162
Victoria TX 77902

https://www.chax.org/

Poems from this manuscript have appeared in *Aufgabe, Best Experimental Writing 2016, Brooklyn Rail, La fovea, Poetry, Pinwheel,* and *Yew*.

This book is for Andrea Baker.

I was thinking the other day that a name for my disease could be empathy, and I looked it up in the dictionary to see if I really knew what it meant. And there was this amazing duality between that and your schizophrenia. It said, "An imaginative projection of one's own consciousness into another person's being."

—Jim Campbell

Mark has two watches,
and I love both of them.

One is black: the other is chrome.
Mark wears one of the two watches at all times

unless painting or asleep.
The watches are quiet but emotional.

The watches are busy and hard
to pin down but they are quite sexy.

The watches are exact but always late.

Jennifer dreamt that her dharma teacher
held her in his arms, and it was sex and

not sex. This occurred in Albuquerque.
Jennifer's dharma teacher confessed that

he had been arrested for PCP use the day before,
and, as a consequence, his bicycle was missing.

Jennifer was confused by her dharma teacher's mixed messages.
There was a swimming pool in the dream also.

Sometimes people called the house and asked
for Jennifer, but it was the wrong Jennifer.

The other Jennifer was much older and
more famous, a painter.

The two Jennifers shared some facts:
they both lived in Brooklyn, and they

both had a fixation on swimming pools.
The other Jennifer had one such swimming pool

in her loft before moving to Brooklyn.
Real Jennifer's husband would

not allow her to have her own
swimming pool.

Mark liked to introduce the real Jennifer
as the other, more famous, Jennifer.

Mark was a painter,
and Mark's friends were painters,

and Mark was highly amused
by the mistaken identity.

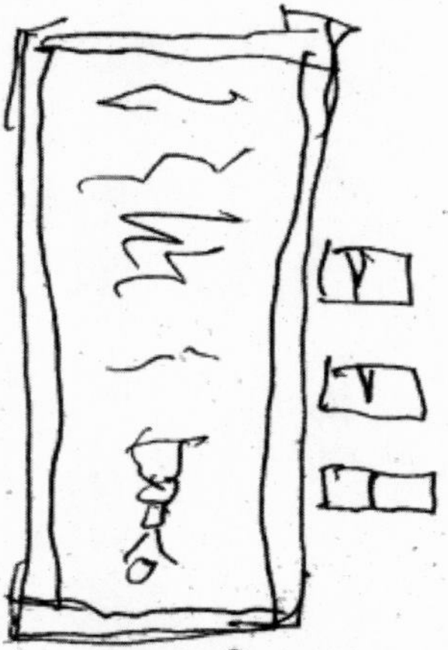

JENNIFER BARTLETT'S Swimming POOL

REAL JENNIFER'S Swimming POOL

Jennifer had a tendency to stop in
the street and listen to the neighbors'

problems. She was consoling to them.
Jennifer would look for people in trouble

and offer help even though
her body was relatively weak, and

she could not carry groceries
for the old people, really.

When the young mothers had issues
they would come to Jennifer because they

knew that Jennifer also had had issues
as a young mother and would listen to them.

Now, Jennifer had middle mother issues.

This Jennifer was not a good Jennifer.
This Jennifer had fallen in love with a married man;

she had, despite everything,
kissed this married man in a wine bar

one day in August.

She had had this married man over to her
house on his 52th birthday and taken off

all his clothes, except his socks, and put
her mouth everywhere on this married man.

This was before she loved him,
and now she loved him, and this was

her conundrum. She suspected the married man
loved her too, but he was from Minnesota,

and Minnesotans don't say such things.

Everything can be illuminated by water
or most things.

The two women in the black of mourning
knelt by the river in exact tandem, and

they spoke softly.
The film, like life itself, had minimal

plot and extraordinary beauty.
The film, like life itself, was

slow and maniacal. And when
we walked the village afterwards

in search of just the right martini
I thought of the same steps I had

taken years earlier in preparation
for mourning, and I was not unhappy.

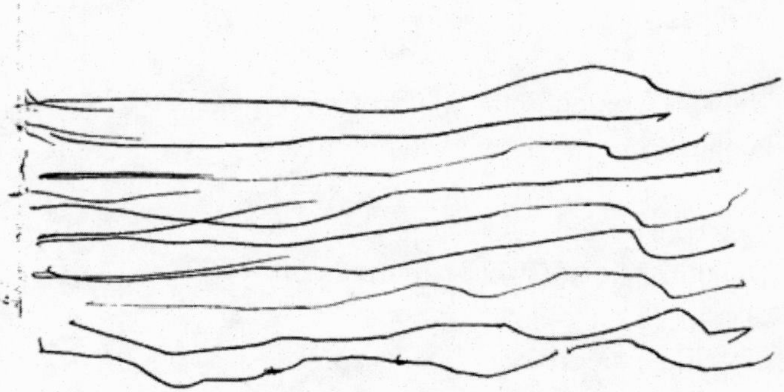

The best thing about the film was
nature as musical score.

In the morning the birds were so loud;
they spoke in patterns.

A mother's writing needs to be fragmented
when children inhabit the room:

a word here, a word there.

Like Robert Musil's "A Man With No Qualities,"
my heart has no qualities.

Dear Mark,

So, you've met my kraken.
Everyone in our house has one.

Mine comes out less and less as
I do a pretty good job of keeping

her at bay. But, sometimes, if pushed enough,
she needs to come up for air.

The other people and animals
in my house are terrified of her.

Only my closest friends have met her,
my family, James knows her well,

and as do a few random poets
on the internet.

Since you have been honest
in letting me know that I am merely

"like your therapist," I figure you
owe me about $5000.

I will take that in art.
My address is 136 Freeman St.

Apt 1A Brooklyn, NY 11222.
Send my Paul Auster book too.

Like all of Jennifers, Jennifer had
a best friend. This best friend was called

Andrea. Andrea and Jennifer discussed
many things. They discussed childrearing

and husbands and boyfriends
and potential husbands and boyfriends.

They discussed philosophy and memoirs
and the best subway routes.

They discussed al-non and Buddhism:
disability and the mom-po list;

Portland poets and food.
They discussed Jennifer's alcoholism

and Jennifer's outfits and
Jennnifer's reluctance to be in the world.

They discussed Andrea's pot habit
and Andrea's family and homeschooling

and television.
They discussed neurology and

the right side of Andrea's body and
eating meat versus not eating meat.

They discuss rape and abortion and
being sexualized versus being desexualized.

They discussed Larry Eigner and Jennifer's
garden and what she should do about it.

They discussed how the neighbor stole Andrea's bike
and sold it and what she should do about that.

They discussed chandeliers and mirrors
and clothes they landed at the thrift store.

They discussed AWP and why you can't use a
cell phone on an airplane and the price of

hotel rooms and pets and Jennifer's husband's
girlfriend and being an artist versus a poet.

They discussed meditation and their dharma teacher
and common household cleaning products

and which was the best public library branch.
They discussed college versus no college

and grants and business plans
and swimming pools and yoga.

They discussed the projects of others and
what it would take to get a teaching job.

They traded ideas and books and
groceries and clothes. They traded

sorrows and worries and happinesses
and printer paper. Andrea could do

things that Jennifer could not do,
and she did some of these things for her.

Conversely, Jennifer did things for Andrea;
things that Andrea did not know how to do.

He is my true friend in the sense that he deeply
cares, I mean, deeply does not care, who I am.

An ABSTRACT with Andrea BOWS on her toes.

Anne had a friend.
This friend was called Rosemary.

Rosemary was an Indian.
Yes. That is what they call themselves: Rosemary.

Rosemary needed to raise a turtle for the
Annual Easter Turtle Race. She kept the

turtle at Anne and Lee's house
in order to keep it secret from

the other Indians raising other turtles for the race.
I am not recalling the turtle's name

just now. Lee left the little turtle vegetables,
but the little turtle hibernated

and did not eat the vegetables.
However, it resurfaced on Easter

exactly according to plan.
Would Rosemary's turtle win the race?

(TUTU)
(LEE)
COME OUT!
LITTLE TURTLE!
SOPHIE
BABY

Jennifer of the boyfriends who hate her.
Jennifer of the hospice for dying animals.

Jennifer of the reading glasses.
Jennifer of the poems.

Jennifer of the love for the married man.
Jennifer of compassion and empathy.

Jennifer of argumentativeness.
Jennifer of the loaded pistol.

Jennifer of the smoking gun.
Jennifer of the hiding.

Jennifer of loss.
Jennifer of letting go.

Jennifer of the Emma and Dion and
James and Tori and Carol.

Jennifer of the Jim and Andrea and
Jeffrey and Nancy and Joel.

Jennifer of the books.

Jennifer thought of emailing Kenzo.
This might take some digging.

She had long ago (years)
thrown all their letters in the trash,

and Kenzo wasn't on social media.
She could kind of remember the first

three numbers of Kenzo's phone number,
but this was not helpful.

She planned to tell Kenzo:
when I met you, I was not

available, but now I am and
this is partially your fault.

My family is out of town and my
best friend is distracted so I have

trouble getting healthy meals. I am
calling because I want you

to come over and make me dinner
and let me blow you as many times as we can bear it.

ear Mark,

You told me that you had many
problems. Among them was

that you did not know what
"in love" meant. You must

know what "in love" does not mean
for some reason because you

were able to tell me that you are
not "in love" with me.

How can you not know what something means,
and yet know what it does not mean?

Eh?

Jennifer told Andrea that men were
easy to get, you just had to decide

that you wanted one. Or in Jennifer's
case, several.

Jennifer imagined herself
much to be like her paternal

grandmother. Marion, a Minnesotan
in every sense of the word, passed

away when Jennifer was six years old.
Marion was a true lady. A cocktail

drinker, a neat freak, Jennifer's
father was not allowed to have animals

as animals were dirty. Perhaps
that is why he had so many animals

as an adult. And Jennifer had
many animals as an adult, as well.

How many things could she do at
once? She raised a boy, she cared

for four animals, she cleaned,

she did errands, she loved,

she hated. She carved a path
from Andrea's house to her

house and back again. She did
this despite the hole in her shoe.

She did magical things, and
she did mundane things.

She studied birds and trees.
She flirted with boys and drank liquor.

She read books and slept. She wondered
who would win the essay contest

at the Ukrainian Institute. She wondered
about the men who worked at the Iraqi

Consulate. Despite the wars, men
always seem relatively cheery, although

they often had trouble keeping their parking space.

Iraqi Consulate
Hey! You can't park there!

This is a poem about lying. This is a poem
about art and artists. Painters, I mean.

This is a poem about fishing and fishermen
and Minnesota. This is a poem about Andrea.

This is a poem about sex. This is poem based on
a poem based on a novel by Gertrude Stein.

This is a poem about objects and language.
When I say objects, I mean Andrea.

She imagined him telling the next one
about her as he had told her about

the previous one. She imagined him
kissing her as he had kissed the previous

one. She imagined him holding hands
with the future one as he had held hands

with her. She imagined him putting
his hand up the skirt of the future

one near the river as he had put
his hand up her skirt near the river

and up the skirt of the previous one.
She imagined him not telling the future

one nor the past one that he loved them
just as he had not told her he loved her

not in their bar, nor the house, nor by the river.
She imagined him putting his fingers

inside of the others: the future, past and present
as he had put his fingers inside of her.

She imagined him lying to the previous ones, the future ones, and the current ones.

But some of the facts were also true.

It was A Good Time

I Rode the subway with CHARLES BERNSTEIN

This was VERY Odd

I forgot to tell him About the dream!

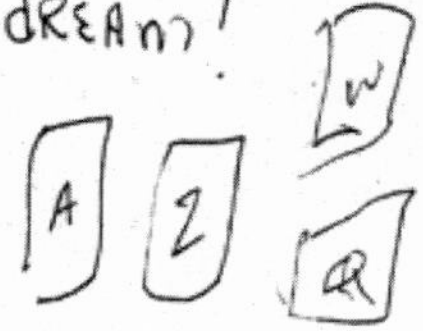

Him & Susan Bee Had A Rather lg APARTMENT...

I a
to
APPL
betw
ALL
ther
Bool

Sometimes it was a green cap.
Sometimes it was a two-year-old blond baby boy.
Sometimes it was a bicycle.
Sometimes it was the pink and black textured wallpaper at
Sweetleaf coffee shop.
Sometimes it was the coffee itself.
Sometimes it was a watch.
Sometimes it was a wedding ring.
Sometimes it was a beautiful, intense woman with
salt and pepper hair.
Sometimes it was the children's park.
Sometimes it was the homeless cats at the river.
Sometimes it was the number 104.
Sometimes it was a pair of shorts.
Sometimes it was abstract painting.
Sometimes it was a pencil factory.
Sometimes it was a beer.
Sometimes it was a name.
Sometimes it was Montauk.
Sometimes it was the ocean.

Today was James 31st
birthday so she would write the poem,

the poem of today; James' 31st birthday.
The following Saturday, the day of James' wedding,

would be Mark's birthday. Mark was 22 years
older than James, nearly to the day.

This would mean that the day James was
born, Mark was married (or nearly married)

to Jean and Mark owned (or nearly owned)
a house and had surely finished college

though not graduate school.
Mark's mother wanted him to

"do something useful" and by this
she did not mean paint.

This all occurred in Minnesota
naturally, which was also where Bob grew up.

The day James was born was also
the day that Jean-Michel Basquiat

died. However, this was in 1988,
so, in reality, it was James' fourth birthday.

Connie knew Jean-Michel because
she worked at the Great Jones Diner,

and Jean-Michel used to
come in and trade things for drinks.

By "things" I mean art.

When I write I think about Lisa Jarnot. When I write I
think about Andrea.

When I write I think about Kate Greenstreet: I think
about Matt Hendrickson. I think about the

Making of the Americans. I think about
the Russian-Turkish Baths and dreams

of the Russian-Turkish baths;
I mean the Boris and Natasha baths.

When I write I think about Mark's two watches
and grilled cheese sandwiches.

When I write, I think about Duncan and Eigner
and Bob. When I think about Bob

I think about Minnesota. I mean
Minneapolis. I mean Mark. I mean

rivers and rivers; an entire state of rivers.
An entire state named after

saints, rivers named after saints,
and saints named after rivers.

Every few weeks she met Saint Jim in the park.
She just wanted to get on Saint Jim's bed and float

away; the bed which happened to be on the same
street as her beloved Mark. But, Saint Jim was

difficult and recalcitrant as is often the
case with saints. So, for now she had to be

happy with their short walks and discussions
of New York, October light, tiny animals, and politics.

Saint Jim told her *don't you dare put me in a poem*
as he tried to feed a squirrel an acorn.

If I cut my body in half, vertically,
words would come pouring out.

If I cut my body in half, I would
have to cut vertically, I would need

really big scissors to do this
and fishes would pour out.

Jennifer and Joel had many things in common.
Both their names began with the letter J.

They were both a little too fond of alcoholic beverages.
They were both kind of slutty or at least

pretended to be kind of slutty. Joel had a small girl
somewhere inside him. Jennifer had

a big man somewhere inside her, hence
the conversation could turn a variety

of ways. They both loved Mark.
Joel loved Mark in one way — a

fishing buddy sort of way;
Jennifer loved Mark in different way—

a kissy girl sort of way.
Mark annoyed Joel and Jennifer in a similar way.

Joel loved his wife Helen in one way, and
Jennifer loved Helen in a different way.

But, they both found her to be entirely illuminous.
I mean luminous. Illuminous is not a word.

AN
ABSTRACT
OF
THE ABBY

He always talked about his exes with his currents
as he had talked about his exes with her:

these included, but were not limited to,
his current wife, his ex-wife, and the lover with short hair

and glasses who thought Joel was hot. She reminded
him of her because she also had short hair,

she sometimes wore glasses and definitely
thought Joel was hot. The opera singer. The one he

met walking to the swimming pool. The one on
craigslist who came to the loft. The one he had

hot sex with but nothing in common. There
weren't that many, six, ten? Most of them

one night stands. One or two were fictional, surely.

She could only imagine what he might say about
her. She was a poet. She to liked write poems about herself

in the third person. She was fiery. Today is her
birthday. We fought a lot, and I don't like fighting

I mean it used to be I couldn't fight at all and
now I can a little. My favorite thing about her

was that she would say something and look away
and look back and pause. She looked like a gazelle.

We both looked like gazelles. I told her (insert lie
here) and that (insert lie here too). Our song was

(blank) by Roxy Music. She told me don't ever
lie to me because I will know. We broke up

because (insert what you remember to be true here).
It was just casual, I mean (insert relative truth here).

What I really mean is:

She looked down
AT a puddLE.
THERE WERE fish
in There.

Joel found a blue boat, and he tore the blue boat apart.
Joel painted boys on the remnants, and he called

these boys swamp boys, and they were beautiful;
Joel's swamp boys.

If I cut myself from within, vertically,
fishes would come pouring out.

If the fishes poured out there could
be no more paintings of the ocean.

This would mean no more swamp boys;
no more paintings on the fragmented

blue boat wood; no more boats.

My body is an ocean.
Connie's mind, too, is an ocean.

We ride the waves of our oceans.

ar Mark

You want to just be happy and
laugh together. Evidently,

I am making it hard to
do that. When I walked away from

the computer you typed in,
Jennifer?

This was the first time said my
name. I didn't even know if you knew it.

Joel made Jennifer cry.
Joel made Jennifer (or Jen as he called her)

cry in the Pencil Factory.
This was not a factory,

and they did not make pencils,
but it was across the street from a

factory (now studios) that had once
made pencils, not far from the factory

that had once made ropes. Joel,
poor Joel, it was just days before

his wedding to Helen. The best man
had injured himself, severely, in a biking accident,

and now Jennifer was in the Pencil Factory,
what I mean is the bar named after

the building that had been a factory
for pencils, crying, for he had told her

that Mark was potentially having an affair
with that painter they had seen at the opening

the week previous. O, Joel,
this was not among your brightest ideas.

HELEN Said
JOEL & JENNifer
NEEDED TIME
APART, OR IT
WAS IMPLIED,
STRONGLY.

r Mark,

I wish I have saved your emails
so that I could put all the

stupid things you said to me
in this poem. You said some nice

things too, I guess.

Mark,

James believes that one should
not use “dear” when writing a letter

because “dear” implies that the person
is dear to you.

They might not be dear:
they might be a colleague, a stranger

or you might just not like them.

Jennifer's problem was that everyone wanted her
to be a certain way. Mark wanted her to be one

way. The feminists wanted her to be another way.
The poets wanted her to be a certain way,

and Lee wanted her to be an alternate way, of
course, contradictory to the first three ways.

Andrea just wanted her to wear socks.
Joel's only real opinion was that they not

eat the fish caught in the East River because
the fish caught in the East River has a very

high mercury content, and Joel saw this as
a problem even though Joel said

the ocean also had a high mercury content,
and Joel ate that fish, happily.

ark,

Lee of the turtle told me not to talk to you.
So did Jim and Joel and Saint Jim.

Bill also told me not to talk to you.
So did my therapist and the librarians

and the fish and the river,
the cats and the birds. Andrea told me not to talk to

you. By talk, I mean "words" via any form
of communication, other than telepathy,

from me to you.

rk,

I will never forget a poem that Kostas wrote
about the girl who broke up with him.

He said, that girl broke up with me,
and if that wasn't enough, she wrote

a ten-page letter telling him everything
that was wrong with him and left it on his doorstep.

k,

Here is everything that is wrong
with you.

You are secretive and you lie, like, all the time.
You do not read enough.

You are always late if you show up; you have a habit
of canceling plans at the last minute.

Sometimes you leave parties without saying goodbye,
and you think this is funny. It is not.

You dress like an aging bicycle messenger.
You use the incorrect prepositions: for example,

you say "of" when you mean by "or"
"to" when you mean "for," and so on and so forth.

You are cheap with money. You are neurotic.
You complain about everything. All the time.

You never call people by their names, and
that is weird. You probably drink too much.

Your mother is a Methodist.
And that's another thing. You always

say, "And that's another thing" whether
or not there is actually a first thing.

You have terrible eyesight, and
on the telephone, you sound like a character

from Fargo. That is when you pick up the telephone,
which you do not. Often. Well, ever.

After a little research, Jennifer
found out that Marion was

actually raised in Winona.
After a little research,

Jennifer could still not tell
whether her paternal grandfather,

who was not from Winona, was
part Indian, as Lee had suggested.

However, she did have one piece of information;
Rosemary's turtle won the race.

Rosemary's turtle, whose name escapes me just now,
would always, always win the race.

Today I awoke full of such mourning.
Not, as you know, only for you, but

for all my loss.
I am everyone's favorite Elizabeth

Bishop poem (besides the one about fishing,
and I am that one too).

I took a taxi across the 59th street Bridge
and looked toward your bike path.

They say that in the journey
to enlightenment anger is the first thing to go.

I, too, am a person who is deeply flawed.
For example, it must be odd to get so many

emails in couplets. The least I could have
done is put them in iambic pentameter.

Will you forgive ever me?
Mark?

About the Author

Jennifer Bartlett is the author of three previous books of poetry including another Chax title, *(a) lullaby without any music*. Bartlett also co-edited *Beauty is a Verb: The New Poetry of Disability* with Sheila Black and Michael Northen. She is currently writing a biography on the poet Larry Eigner.

CHAX

Founded in 1984 in Tucson, Arizona, Chax has published 200 books in a variety of formats, including hand printed letterpress books and chapbooks, hybrid chapbooks, book arts editions, and trade paperback editions such as the book you are holding. In August 2014 Chax moved to Victoria,Texas, and is presently located in the University of Houston-Victoria Center for the Arts. UHV has generously supported the publication of *The Hindrances of a Householder*, a book that has also received support from many friends of the press. Chax is an independent 501(c)(3) organization that depends on support from various government and private funders, and, primarily, from individual donors and readers.

Recent books from Chax include *Diesel Hand*, by Nico Vassilakis, *Entangled Bank*, by James Sherry, *Autocinema*, by Gaspar Orozco, *The Letters of Carla, the letter b.*, by Benjamin Hollander, *Artifice in the Calm Damages*, by Andrew Levy, *Any Would Be If*, by Norman Fischer, *Leaves of Class*, by Kit Robinson, *A Night in the Sun*, by Will Alexander, *Visible Instruments*, by Michael Kelleher, and *A Mere Rica*, by Linh Dinh. Books in the works include titles by David Dowker, Tracie Morris, Serge Gavronsky, Beverly Dahlen, and Hélène Sanguinetti (trans. by Ann Cefola), among others.

You may find CHAX online at *http://chax.org*